Kissing Frogs
and
Trying on Shoes

A Study to Help Teen Girls Navigate the Dating
World and Develop Their Identity in Christ

Michele Corgiat

Copyright © 2016 Michele Corgiat.

All rights reserved. No part of this book may be used or reproduced by any means, graphic, electronic, or mechanical, including photocopying, recording, taping or by any information storage retrieval system without the written permission of the author except in the case of brief quotations embodied in critical articles and reviews.

Scripture taken from the King James Version of the Bible.

Scripture taken from the Holy Bible, New International Version®. Copyright © 1973, 1978, 1984 Biblica. Used by permission of Zondervan. All rights reserved.

Scripture quotations are from The Holy Bible, English Standard Version® (ESV®), copyright © 2001 by Crossway, a publishing ministry of Good News Publishers. Used by permission. All rights reserved.

WestBow Press books may be ordered through booksellers or by contacting:

WestBow Press
A Division of Thomas Nelson & Zondervan
1663 Liberty Drive
Bloomington, IN 47403
www.westbowpress.com
1 (866) 928-1240

Because of the dynamic nature of the Internet, any web addresses or links contained in this book may have changed since publication and may no longer be valid. The views expressed in this work are solely those of the author and do not necessarily reflect the views of the publisher, and the publisher hereby disclaims any responsibility for them.

Any people depicted in stock imagery provided by Thinkstock are models, and such images are being used for illustrative purposes only. Certain stock imagery © Thinkstock.

ISBN: 978-1-4908-9580-2 (sc)
ISBN: 978-1-4908-9581-9 (e)

Library of Congress Control Number: 2015915462

Print information available on the last page.

WestBow Press rev. date: 03/22/2016

Dedicated to the Fathers in my life

To My Heavenly Father

May I always be in the middle of Your will and
be used by You in whatever way You wish.

To My Earthly Father

Thank you for being an awesome example of God's love for me.

To My Husband and Father of My Children

Thank you for your support and encouragement
in my career and for our family.

About the Author

Michele Corgiat received her Masters of Arts degree from Azusa Pacific University and began her career in counseling working with teen boys and girls in group homes. She now has a private practice in Modesto, California as a licensed Marriage and Family Therapist providing counseling services to children, teens and adults. Michele has been serving the Lord since age 5 and continues to seek His will in her life. Several years ago she asked God to begin using her passion for Christian counseling. She describes this time in her life like being a horse waiting in the gates for a race to begin. Once God "opened the gate", she has experienced a wild ride that only God could have designed.

Michele is married and mother of two boys. Her ministry begins at home with her family but God has been faithful in allowing her the time and flexibility to reach out and help others experience healthy relationships and develop their identities in Christ.

Contents

About the Author.................................... vii

Introduction..xi

WEEK 1:
　Kissing Frogs and Trying on Shoes...................... 1

WEEK 2:
　You are a Pearl 15

WEEK 3:
　Don't give your pearls to a pig!....................... 27

WEEK 4:
　Don't be a vampire girl............................. 37

WEEK 5:
　Twitterpated vs. love............................... 47

WEEK 6:
　How do you get back on track if you already took the wrong road?....................................... 59

Introduction

Welcome to the world of dating and relationships. As we grow into lovely young ladies, we sometimes don't feel so lovely. In fact, we often feel ugly on the inside and the outside. We experience confusion over friends and boys. How do we get a boyfriend? How do we find happiness in relationships? Do relationships have to be full of drama? Do we have to do things that may compromise our value systems?

This bible study is designed to help you navigate through developing healthy relationships and forming your identity through God's eyes. Weekly, you will be able to explore different aspects of relationships such as identifying what the world is telling you about dating, different kinds of boys you should stay away from, how to act and not act in relationships, and developing your wish list for the "perfect guy". We will also explore what love is through God's eyes and how to love the person that God has created in you.

Whether you are working through this study on your own, in a small group, or a counseling setting, this study is designed to encourage you to process through some of your own views and beliefs and compare them to the Truths found in God's Word. Each daily lesson, individually titled, will include scriptural references and end with "Thoughts of the day". God wants you to take His Word very personally. I pray that every day you will find that He is speaking directly to you!

I invite you to comment online on my website:

http://counselingmchl.community.officelive.com/
KissingFrogsandTryingonShoes.aspx

Or join the conversation on Facebook page:

Kissing Frogs and Trying on Shoes

WEEK 1:

Day 1
Kissing Frogs and Trying on Shoes

What was your favorite love story? Was it Cinderella? Beauty and the Beast? Twilight? I saw a classic movie in junior high school and I loved it. It was called "An Affair to Remember". It's about a man and a woman who meet on a cruise ship traveling from England to New York. They fall in love but are both in other relationships. They choose not to do anything they will regret, so they plan to put some space and time between each other. If their love is "real", they will both show up at the top of the Empire State Building in six months to get married. Of course, there is drama. He shows up, but she does not. Our Hero is devastated and goes on a journey to "find himself". (This would not be a good story if it were too easy). Through a series of events, the hero of our story, once again, finds his love. His true love had, in fact, gone to the Empire State Building on that fateful day, only to be a victim of a traffic accident that left her without the use of her legs. In the end, he accepts her and her limitations and they live happily ever after. This story has romance, drama, tragedy, and resolution. If we could only write out our own romance stories to always have a happy ending! Fortunately, there is not a Hollywood writer helping us along in our own fairy tales. We have God planning our future for us.

In 2004, Young and Modern Magazine had a survey that reported 80% of teens listed dating or having a boyfriend as their top desire. We want the love story in our own lives. We are each longing to be noticed, pursued, and loved forever and unconditionally. The problem is we don't know how, where, who, or when? When we look for answers to those questions, we often don't feel comfortable in talking to our parents, or our parents don't feel comfortable talking to us! Seventeen Magazine reported that 95% of teens never discussed kissing, making out and other sexual contact with their moms. If we aren't talking to our moms, then where do we get those answers from?

Hollywood, music, friends, and magazines are all so very willing to answer your questions for you. They are all jumping up and down, trying to get your attention! If you listen very carefully you can hear the messages that they are saying. "You need to look this way or that way to be accepted, you need to be sexy, the only way to be happy is to have a hot guy in your life, the way to keep a guy is by putting out, and you are worthless if you don't follow these rules." Most of those lies have us paying a lot of money to look and act older during our teenage years and then trying to look and act younger after we turn 30. It has generations of women trying to "hook-up" with a guy to find happiness and fulfillment. I know it's sometimes difficult to accept that these are lies because they are everywhere and so many have bought into the lies. I guarantee that they will not bring you happiness, peace, or contentment. Instead you will experience pain, conflict, sadness and discontent if you choose to buy into these lies.

Read I Corinthians 6:9

*Do you not know that the wicked will not inherit the kingdom of God? Do not be **deceived**: Neither the sexually immoral nor idolaters nor adulterers nor male prostitutes nor homosexual offenders*[a]

And verses 19-20

[9] Do you not know that your body is a temple of the Holy Spirit, who is in you, whom you have received from God? You are not your own; [20] you were bought at a price. Therefore honor God with your body.

[b]*Thought of the day:*
What lies have you bought into regarding dating or relationships?

_____

_____

---

a   *The Holy Bible: New International Version.* electronic ed. Grand Rapids : Zondervan, 1996, c1984, S. 1 Co 6:9
b   *The Holy Bible: New International Version.* electronic ed. Grand Rapids : Zondervan, 1996, c1984, S. 1 Co 6:19-20

Take some time to look at where you've been in relationships and where you want to go and write **your** Hollywood story or Fairy Tale:

_____
_____
_____
_____
_____
_____
_____
_____
_____

Day 2
Trying on shoes

I don't know about you, but I love to shop for shoes. So many choices of style, color, price, height…. I'm smiling just thinking about it! Could you imagine if you went into a store to buy shoes and the storekeeper announced that you had to buy the first pair you tried on? I'm so glad that this is not the case. What fun would that be? Well, I am also so glad to say that the first boy you meet is most likely not your soul mate. There are those couples that meet in the first grade and are married for 60 years but most often this isn't the case.

God created Eve specifically for Adam.
Read Genesis 2:20-22.

> So the man gave names to all the livestock, the birds of the air and all the beasts of the field.
>
> But for Adam[a] no suitable helper was found. ²¹ So the LORD God caused the man to fall into a deep sleep; and while he was sleeping, he took one of the man's ribs[b] and closed up the place with flesh. ²² Then the LORD God made a woman from the rib[c] he had taken out of the man, and he brought her to the man.

What was Adam missing (v. 20)? _____

What did God do for Adam? (v. 21-22) _____

I love that God made Eve to be a helper to Adam. Our role is part of God's plan. God knew Adam's needs and desires because he made Adam. God also made you. He knows your needs and your desires. You may think you know what kind of guy you want, but remember God knows you better than you know yourself, and he will bring the right individual

---

a   Or *the man*
b   Or *took part of the man's side*
c   Or *part*

to stand by your side. Just like you sometimes have to try on different pairs of shoes to find the right fit, you may have to date a few guys to find God's best fit for you.

Read Psalms 139:1-4
O Lord, You have searched me and known me. You know my sitting down and my rising up; You understand my thought afar off. You comprehend my path and my lying down, And are acquainted with all my ways. For there is not a word on my tongue, But behold, O Lord, You know it altogether.

Thought of the day:
Do you find it difficult or easy to give this choice over to God?

_____

_____

Identify some stumbling blocks you have in giving control over to God?

Day 3
Is dating ever fun?

Sometimes, yes… and sometimes, no. Dating seems to be filled with fun, romance, drama, and heartache. I'm thrilled that dating doesn't have to be drama. We as women are usually the one's creating the drama, but we will talk more about this later on in our study. Romance will also be discussed later, but I will say that romance is often what makes dating happen. It's that "twitterpated feeling" that tells us we are attracted to a guy. What about the fun? Dating can be a lot of fun if this is what you set as an expectation for yourself. We each place expectations on individuals and experiences throughout our lives. If you place an expectation on dating that you are going to have fun, you most likely will attract guys and be attracted to guys that also want to have fun. My question for you is what kind of fun do you want to have? If you are choosing to live a relationship with Christian, then I would encourage you to choose your fun wisely. Staying away from situations that are going to cause temptation that is physically inappropriate is always a good idea.

Read Proverbs 7:7-27
I saw among the simple,
I noticed among the young men,
a youth who lacked judgment.
⁸ He was going down the street near her corner,
walking along in the direction of her house
⁹ at twilight, as the day was fading,
as the dark of night set in.
¹⁰ Then out came a woman to meet him,
dressed like a prostitute and with crafty intent.
¹¹ (She is loud and defiant,
her feet never stay at home;
¹² now in the street, now in the squares,
at every corner she lurks.)

¹³ She took hold of him and kissed him
and with a brazen face she said:
¹⁴ "I have fellowship offerings ᵃ at home;
today I fulfilled my vows.
¹⁵ So I came out to meet you;
I looked for you and have found you!
¹⁶ I have covered my bed
with colored linens from Egypt.
¹⁷ I have perfumed my bed
with myrrh, aloes and cinnamon.
¹⁸ Come, let's drink deep of love till morning;
let's enjoy ourselves with love!
¹⁹ My husband is not at home;
he has gone on a long journey.
²⁰ He took his purse filled with money
and will not be home till full moon."
²¹ With persuasive words she led him astray;
she seduced him with her smooth talk.
²² All at once he followed her
like an ox going to the slaughter,
like a deer ᵇ stepping into a noose ᶜ
²³ till an arrow pierces his liver,
like a bird darting into a snare,
little knowing it will cost him his life.
²⁴ Now then, my sons, listen to me;
pay attention to what I say.
²⁵ Do not let your heart turn to her ways
or stray into her paths.
²⁶ Many are the victims she has brought down;
her slain are a mighty throng.
²⁷ Her house is a highway to the grave,ᵈ
leading down to the chambers of death. ᵉ

---

a   Traditionally *peace offerings*
b   Syriac (see also Septuagint); Hebrew *fool*
c   The meaning of the Hebrew for this line is uncertain.
d   Hebrew *Sheol*
e   *The Holy Bible: New International Version*. electronic ed. Grand Rapids : Zondervan, 1996, c1984, S. Pr 7:7-27

How does this scripture describe this young man (v. 7)?
_____
_____

Who is tempting him (v. 10)?
_____
_____

How does she seduce him? (v.21)
_____
_____

Temptation is everywhere. We are told by TV, music, magazines and the world in general that we are to be sexy, lusty, and tempting to the opposite sex. The good news is God made us naturally attractive to the opposite sex . Eve didn't need make-up, push up bras, or even shave her legs to make herself more attractive to Adam. He made guys so they want us! It's up to us girls to help the guy out in his battle with temptation and not give the idea that we are merely about the sexy and lusty.

Read 2 Timothy 2:22
> *Flee also youthful lusts; but pursue righteousness, faith, love, peace with those who call on the Lord out of a pure heart.*

Thought of the day:
What are ways that you have tried to present yourself as sexy or seductive?
_____
_____

If you leave seduction out of it, what traits do you **want** guys to see in you and what traits **are** they seeing in you?
_____
_____

Day 4
Beauty is as beauty does

I once had a young lady ask me, "why is it that the guys I like don't like me, and the guys who like me, I don't like". Some cultures still match up couples through matchmakers or by arranged marriages between families. I remember thinking in college that I was not having much luck on my own and maybe these cultures had it right. Today we are going to address the art of flirting, letting the guy you like know in an "appropriate way" that you are interested. What do we do? What do we say? We often become so unsure of ourselves that we resort to dressing and acting in ways that don't really represent who we are, in order to get a guys attention. Or, in sharp contrast, we clam up and become a wallflower that doesn't know how to talk to a guy and even runs from a room if one approaches.

God has given you gifts and talents. One may be a talented athlete who has the gift of humor, while another may be talented in music and have the gift of grace. Being comfortable with who you are, is the key to flirting. I will talk a lot about not buying into the world's view of relationships, except in this one case. If you watch a television show and just focus on the characteristics of women who are flirting, though usually inappropriately, they all appear very "sure of themselves".

Here are some questions to think about:
Do you look your friends in the eye when they talk to you, but look away from a guy you like?

_____

_____

Do you actually talk to the guy you like or tell a friend to talk to him?

_____

_____

Do you present yourself in a provocative way in order to get their attention?

_____

_____

I know self-confidence can be difficult to attain, especially at this stage of life. You have been growing up so quickly and are just trying to keep up with yourself. There is that little girl inside screaming, "I have no clue what is going on, and somebody might find out". Would it make you feel better to know that a lot of the guys have that same voice inside?

If you can talk to a guy (as yourself) and just be friendly (without telling your whole life story), he's going to take notice. If you are comfortable and make him feel comfortable you are being successful. Realize, however, that you can't make him, nor do you want to make him like you. If you are meant to take it to the "dating" stage of this fairy tale, then he's going to have to be attracted to you too. Also, remember that you don't always know the whole story. Maybe he likes you but doesn't have time for dating or relationships. Maybe he likes you but doesn't want to sacrifice your friendship. Or maybe he just doesn't see you in the "girlfriend" kind of way. I know that it can be difficult to interrupt the dream of the fairy tale but that doesn't mean your story ends there. It just may be with another prince.

Thought of the day:
How did God make you?

_____

_____

Identify your talents and gifts.

_____

_____

_____

_____

In your journey of "finding yourself", who are you?

_____

_____

Isaiah 43: 7

> *everyone who is called by My name, • whom I **created** for My glory, whom I formed and made."*

Genesis 1:27

> *So God created man in His own image, in the image of God He created him; male and female He created them.* [a]

---

[a] *The Holy Bible: New International Version.* electronic ed. Grand Rapids : Zondervan, 1996, c1984, S. Ge 1:27

Day 5
Kissing frogs

There are many parents and pastors who teach their daughters not to kiss a boy until they get married. I'm being realistic that most of you will likely kiss a boy or two (or three or four) before you get married. Many of today's teens are not just kissing the boys, they are having sex. 46.8% of all teens report that they have had sexual intercourse. There is a saying that you have to kiss a lot of frogs before you find a prince. I promise that you don't have to kiss any frogs, and you definitely don't have to have sex with any, in order to find your prince.

Read I Corinthians 6:18-20

> [8] *Flee from sexual immorality. All other sins a man commits are outside his body, but he who sins sexually sins against his own body.* [19] *Do you not know that your body is a temple of the Holy Spirit, who is in you, whom you have received from God? You are not your own;* [20] *you were bought at a price. Therefore honor God with your body.* [a]

What are you sinning against when you commit sexual immorality (v. 18)?

_____

_____

According to verses 19 and 20, our bodies are temples of the Holy Spirit. God indwells each of us when we ask him into our lives! He also bought us at a price. He died on the cross for you and me so that we can be with Him for eternity. The great news is that we don't have to wait until we are in heaven to be with Him. He has sent His Holy Spirit to be with us.

---

a *The Holy Bible: New International Version.* electronic ed. Grand Rapids : Zondervan, 1996, c1984, S. 1 Co 6:18-20

Thought of the day:
Do you feel like you are in the trap of kissing frogs?
_____
_____

What choices have gotten you into this trap?
_____
_____

Have you asked God to be in control of your whole life?
_____
_____

Even you're dating life?
_____
_____

WEEK 2:
YOU ARE A PEARL

Day 1
Growing up a princess! (Vs. a superhero)

Little girls love to be noticed by their daddy's and to be told how pretty and lovely they are. If you go to a children's section of a store, you will even find princess costumes to help a little girl fulfill her princess dreams. When a little girl gets healthy attention from her daddy, she shines brighter than any star. As little girls are nurtured and grow, their daddy's continually remind them through their attention and interactions that they are more precious than any riches the world could provide. They are a like a pearl!

As we grow up, we continue to want to feel precious and lovely and have others see us in this way. We often seek this attention in the young men that we find attractive. I bring this up so that you can stop for a moment and reflect on what you may be getting out of your relationships.

What do you want from these young men in your life?
_____
_____

Do you want companionship, friendship, or do you want somebody to make you feel beautiful?
_____
_____

If you are looking for the latter, I'm afraid to tell you that you are looking in the wrong place.

I think that it's helpful to understand where the guys are coming from. If girls are looking to be princesses, what are boys looking to be? Superheroes!!!!!!!!!!!!! You can go shopping at that same children's section and you will find superhero costumes for the boys. The superhero may change based on what movie is out in theaters, but most often you will find at least one Spiderman or Superman costume. I've known little boys who went everywhere dressed up in their costume and pretended to be that powerful superman. They are looking to be a hero. Later on, as they "mature", boys may lose the costume, but their desire to be that hero remains. I've heard many boys say, "I wish I could be the best at something." Just like the little girl's experience of being a princess can form her expectation of others around her, the little boy's experience of being a superhero, or the "best", can form his expectation of himself. If he was not built up as a little boy and felt that he could do nothing right, he may not see himself capable of being any kind of hero. A boy's self image can be very fragile just like a girl's.

When you look to others on this earth to help you feel beautiful, strong, precious, or heroic, you will always be greatly disappointed. Keep in mind that our moms and dads, who may be wonderful, are also flesh and blood. So are the guys that we seek attention from. They are humans and they are fallen men and women who will never be able to completely fulfill our desires. The only place we can find true beauty and true heroism is through the acceptance of Christ. He sees us as a beautiful creation in Him. It sometimes takes work, however, to view ourselves through God's eyes.

Read *Isaiah* 43:1
> *But now thus says the Lord, he who **created** you, O Jacob, he who formed you, O Israel: "Fear not, for I have redeemed you; I have called you by name, you are mine.* *

Psalm 139:13-14
> *For you created my inmost being; you knit me together in my mother's womb. I praise you because I am fearfully and wonderfully made; your works are wonderful, I know that full well.*

Jeremiah 1:5
> *Before I formed you in the womb I knew you, before you were born I set you apart, I appointed you.*

Thought of the day:
Who has had the greatest impact on how you view yourself?
_____

_____

Do you see yourself as being more lovely because of this person?
_____

_____

Who has made you feel less lovely about yourself?
_____

_____

Day 2
The wounded little girl

What happens when your father or mother haven't been an examples of God's love? How can we view God as all loving, all caring, and all giving if our earthly parents have not been any of those things? I am sad to say that there are many girls out there who have experienced either no relationship with their dad or their relationship has been so messed up that they have been hurt more than helped. That little girl is always with us, searching for our dad's approval and for him to make us feel desired and lovely. We may get a skewed idea of how men treat women, especially if this relationship is characterized by verbal attacks, emotional or sexual abuse. A girl may be getting her father's attention, but it's not developing her into a healthy adult woman. When a child experiences this inappropriate attention, she can easily develop the belief that this is how she is to be treated by men. The kind of love that we seek from our father is a pure and caring love that we can only imagine a parent feels for a child. This is the way of the "Abba Father". You may have heard this term used in churches, but let's look more carefully at what it really means.

Abba (ab'-bah) = Father (denotes childlike intimacy and trust. A title of *great* respect.) [a]

We see Jesus use this term when praying to His Father in Mark 14:36, "*Abba*,[ba] Father," he said, "everything is possible for you. Take this cup from me. Yet not what I will, but what you will." [c] Jesus was faced with certain death, but his father had the ability to change the outcome. With childlike trust, Jesus gives up His control and will and let's His Abba Father direct the circumstance while comforting in God's strength.

---

[a] Smith, Stelman; Cornwall, Judson: *The Exhaustive Dictionary of Bible Names*. North Brunswick, NJ : Bridge-Logos, 1998, S. 1
[b] Aramaic for *Father*
[c] *The Holy Bible: New International Version*. electronic ed. Grand Rapids : Zondervan, 1996, c1984, S. Mk 14:36

Read Psalms 23.

> *The Lord is my shepherd; I shall not want.*
> *He makes me to lie down in green pastures:*
> *he leads me beside the still waters.*
> *He restores my soul: he leads me in the paths of*
> *righteousness for his name's sake.*
> *Yeah, though I walk through the valley of the shadow of death, I will fear*
> *no evil: for you are with me: Your rod and Your staff they comfort me.*
> *You prepare a table before me in the presence of my enemies:*
> *You anoint my head with oil; my cup runs over.*
> *Surely goodness and mercy shall follow me all the days of my*
> *life: and I will dwell in the house of the Lord Forever.*

What an awesome thought that the Lord is our father! Psalms 23 is often read at funerals as a comfort to those who are mourning. I think it should be read as a celebration of God's love and comfort to us.

Read the passage again, but this time picture yourself in David's place and emphasize "me" (you may want to read it aloud).

He is the "bestest" Dad ever! He gives us rest, leads us into peace, takes care of and heals our wounds. He protects us and comforts us when we are afraid, feeds us out of His abundance and offers us a home with Him forever. Even if you've never experienced these attributes from an earthly father, God can fulfill this vacancy in your life no matter your age or stage in life.

Thought of the day:
How is the Father that is described in Psalms 23 different from your earthly father?

_____

_____

How is he the same?

_____

_____

If your earthly father has been abusive, you need to let somebody know, such as a counselor, pastor, or teacher. Please know that nobody ever deserves this treatment and that it's ok to seek outside help to end the abuse.

Day 3
Who to Trust?

Romans 8:15-17

⁵ For you did not receive a spirit that makes you a slave again to fear, but you received the Spirit of sonship.ᵃᵍAnd by him we cry, "Abba,ᵇʰ Father." ¹⁶ The Spirit himself testifies with our spirit that we are God's children. ¹⁷ Now if we are children, then we are heirs—heirs of God and co-heirs with Christ, if indeed we share in his sufferings in order that we may also share in his glory.

There is that "Abba Father" title again. I know we hit on this yesterday, but it's such an important concept that we're going to ponder it for just a bit longer. We talked about how Christ called out to his Abba Father as an example of trust. It's not always easy to trust people we can see, let alone trusting a God we can't see.

I remember going on a roller coaster once and being very excited about the ride. The person I was with, however, started freaking out as the roller coaster was going up that first climb. Click, click, click…click…. As we grew closer to the edge, he got more and more fearful. There are times that in relationships we also may grow fearful or anxious. Can we trust this person? Is this person right for me? Am I right for this person? Although the roller coaster of relationships is a great adventure, all of these questions are normal and appropriate. In fact, if you don't ask some of these questions, you may run into some major issues later on. Your roller coaster may derail with very destructive consequences. If you are prayerful about your relationship, asking these questions, and seeking your Abba Fathers answers, you will find peace. Your peace may be with or without that particular guy, but you will find peace.

Finding God's will in our lives, whether it's about a guy or about any decision in life can be challenging. He gives us the freedom of "choice"

---
a   Or *adoption*
b   Aramaic for *Father*

while having the expectation that we will continue to look to Him for guidance.

Psalms 62:6-8

> *He alone is my rock and my salvation;*
> *he is my fortress, I will not be shaken.*
> *⁷ My salvation and my honor depend on God [a];*
> *he is my mighty rock, my refuge.*
> *⁸ Trust in him at all times, O people;*
> *pour out your hearts to him,*
> *for God is our refuge.* [b]

Proverbs 3:5-6

> *Trust in the LORD with all your heart*
> *and lean not on your own understanding;*
> *⁶ in all your ways acknowledge him,*
> *and he will make your paths straight.* [c] [d]

Isaiah 41:10

> *So do not fear, for I am with you;*
> *do not be dismayed, for I am your God.*
> *I will strengthen you and help you;*
> *I will uphold you with my righteous right hand.* [e]

Thought of the day:
What stops you from trusting in God?

_____

_____

Why do we so often give control to God and then take it back?

_____

_____

---

a   Or / *God Most High is my salvation and my honor*
b   *The Holy Bible: New International Version.* electronic ed. Grand Rapids : Zondervan, 1996, c1984, S. Ps 62:6-8
c   Or *will direct your paths*
d   *The Holy Bible: New International Version.* electronic ed. Grand Rapids : Zondervan, 1996, c1984, S. Pr 3:5-6
e   *The Holy Bible: New International Version.* electronic ed. Grand Rapids : Zondervan, 1996, c1984, S. Is 41:10

Day 4
Embracing your Prince

As we continue to search for our "Prince Charming", the hunt can become pretty discouraging. We look for the guy who loves God, loves us, gets along with our family and friends, and understands our life experiences. Girlfriend, you may be hunting for a fantasy! There is one Prince that is out there, however, who fits the bill. His name is Jesus. He is not only our Abba Father, but our King of Kings, Lord of Lords, and Prince of Peace. Yes! I said, "Prince". He will bring you peace, love, understanding, and comfort.

Read Isaiah 9:6

For to us a child is born,
to us a son is given,
and the government will be on his shoulders.
And he will be called
Wonderful Counselor,[a] *Mighty God,*
Everlasting Father, **Prince of Peace**. [b]

In a popular movie for the 90's, there is a famous line, "You complete me". No human is meant to complete us. I know that you will continue to search for Mr. Right, but by embracing Jesus as your prince, you will find fulfillment and be complete in Him. God has a plan for your life. When we are looking to Him, Jesus has a chance to fulfill the best plan, bring those into your life that you need, and give you the desires of your heart.

Read Psalm 37:4

Delight yourself in the Lord
and he will give you the desires of your heart

---
a Or *Wonderful, Counselor*
b *The Holy Bible : New International Version.* electronic ed. Grand Rapids : Zondervan, 1996, c1984, S. Is 9:6

The struggle we often find in embracing God's plan is letting go of our own plan. Our plans can sometimes go like this: After college, I want to get married, have 4 kids (2 boys and twin girls); their names are going to be Jack, Jake, Lily and Lucy. My husband will be tall, like everything I like, not like things I don't like, worship the ground I walk on, and be very wealthy so that we may serve the Lord wherever He may lead us, without financial stress (as long as God's not calling us to a jungle area because I don't do well with humidity).

When we honor God by giving him our plans, will and ultimate control, then He will bless us beyond measure and bring to us contentment.

Read John 5:30
I can of Myself do nothing. As I hear, I judge; and My judgment is righteous, because I do not seek My own will but the will of the Father who sent Me.

Thought of the day:
What is the difference between the plans and the desires of your heart?
_____
_____

What plans have you already made and would you consider letting go of those for God's plan?
_____
_____

Day 5
We are pleased to introduce....you.

Remember the movie that I told you about on the first day of this study? I didn't tell you many details about our hero of the story. The reason he needs to discover "himself" is because his identity was wrapped up in being a "player". In the movie, there are reporters announcing his engagement around the world because he was known as "New York's most eligible bachelor." Sounds kind of like our modern day media. We are so taken up with the comings and goings of music and movie stars. I bet you could find out what Millie Cyrus had for breakfast today if you really wanted to know. But who are we? I wish I had my magic wand and could just presto! Tell you who you were, but this is part of growing up. It too is kind of like trying on shoes. We may try different music styles, explore different interests, take a variety of classes to discover what we like and don't like. During junior high, high school, and college we are finding out what our interests are and melding it to our personalities. Deep stuff, I know. Just wait, I'm only getting started. Not only do we find out what we like, we (hopefully) become more responsible and grow out of the shadow of our families and now become a "me" instead of a "we". Many young people fight for the "me" status while they are still under their parents' roofs. I hate to tell you this but you are still a "we" while you are under your parents' authority. It's not until you are outside their authority that you get "me" status.

I'm going to tread on some thin ice. How about those young ladies who have been dating "the guy" for several years in high school or early college and decide that they want to get married early into their adult years (18-20 years old). They may have a variety of reasons to get married, such as getting out of their parents house, to have guilt free sex or because they think that this is the fairy tale and this is what you do. I would just like to advise you to really think about this step. I cannot tell you how many women in their 30's and 40's have come into my counseling office that got married and started their families very young. They often don't feel like they know who they are as individuals. During the time that they should have been figuring out the "me", they just jumped from one "we" to the next. The great thing is this is one of the decisions in your life that you truly are in control of and have time on your side. I know patience can be one of the most difficult disciplines to master, but you have time. There may be many things that life may throw at you that do not allow any time to adjust to and that you just simply don't have a choice about. Parents announcing they are getting a divorce, being told that you have a life threatening illness, or having a close friend move away. You may not have a choice in any of these types of decisions, so embrace the choices that you do have. To become who God has created you to become.

Romans 8:18
> *[18] I consider that our present sufferings are not worth comparing with the glory that will be revealed in us.[a]*

Be patient for the Glory that is to be revealed!

Thought of the day:
What are some of the choices that have been made for you in your life?
_____
_____

How have some of these choices affected you in a negative way?
_____
_____

How have some of these choices affected you in a positive way?
_____
_____

---

a   *The Holy Bible: New International Version.* electronic ed. Grand Rapids : Zondervan, 1996, c1984, S. Ro 8:18

WEEK 3:
Don't give your pearls to a pig!

Day 1
Swine kind #1: A guy who hurts you

Being hit by a guy or hitting a guy is NEVER okay... I cannot make this point more strongly. If you are being hit, shoved, kicked, or in anyway physically or emotionally threatened or harmed, you need to tell somebody and get out of that relationship. Even if he promises to never do it again, he will if he does not get professional help. Talk to an adult such as a parent, pastor, youth leader, teacher, or counselor. The guy may tell you that it's your fault that you made him that angry. You may tell yourself that you brought up a subject that you knew would bother him. . Let me repeat myself....IT IS NOT OKAY FOR A GUY TO HIT A GIRL!!!!!! EVER!!!!!!!!!!!! If you tell somebody you will be helping him to understand how wrong this is and hopefully get the help he needs. I would encourage any girl to also seek some counsel to make sure that this is not a pattern of the type of guys she is attracted to. Believe it or not, some women are attracted to guys with issues. They don't know they have issues up front, but find out after they are a smitten kitten.

I know that we are not talking about husbands at this time, but we will use a scripture to describe how a husband is to treat his wife.

Read Ephesians 6:25- 33
Husbands, love your wives, just as Christ also loved the church and gave Himself for it, that he might sanctify and cleanse it with the washing of water by the word... (v.28) So husbands aught to love their own wives as their own bodies; he who loves his wife loves himself.... (vs.33) Nevertheless let each one of you in particular so love his own wife as himself, and let the wife see that she respects her husband.

There is so much in these scriptures that I could write a book just on this passage. I just want to highlight a few points. If your guy loves you the way God loves you, he won't hurt you. You are called to respect the man that God has for you. Respect is earned through building trust. How can you trust and respect anybody who treats you with disrespect?

Thought of the day:
Have you or a friend ever been in an abusive relationship? (remember this doesn't have to be physical abuse)
___
___

What is God's desire for you as His daughter?
___
___

Day 2
Swine kind #2: friends with benefits

"Friends with benefits" is a term that has developed over the past decade. What does this mean? Having a physical relationship with somebody who you are not committed to or who is not committed to you. He may be a friend or somebody you once dated. Usually the scenario goes like this.

Girl likes boy.
Boy doesn't want to date or commit to girl (may have different reasons).
Boy wants physical relationship.
Girl thinks she can get boy to like her if she gives boy what he wants
Benefits occur (kissing, making out, sex).
Girl feels bad about self because boy still doesn't want to date her.

You may be asking yourself about now, why would anybody do this? It's back to the fact that young women are not seeing themselves as being precious but want so desperately to find somebody who will help them feel special…no matter the cost. If you are one of these girls, you are not treating yourself with the respect that Christ wants for you. He wants you to feel special. He desires for you to see yourself as a limited edition, rare, hard to find, a precious jewel. There is a high price that has been paid for you. Why does some boy get to throw you away and lower your self-worth?

Read I Corinthians 6:20
> *For you were bought at a price; therefore glorify God in your body and in your spirit, which are God's.*

Thought of the day:
How are you glorifying God in your Body?

_____

_____

Michele Corgiat

How are you glorifying God in your spirit?

_____

_____

_____

_____

_____

Day 3
Swine kind #3: The "player"

The "player" is the guy who seems to be really into you but he also is "into" another girl or even two or three other girls. We've had recent examples of sports stars who participated in this behavior. Having a multitude of "relationships" with women who thought they were the only other woman besides his wife. These are extreme examples of being a player. Most of the guys you will come across, whether it is in high school or college will be dating several girls at a time but will make you feel like he is fully interested in you when he is in your presence. There is a saying, "once a player, always a player". I know that God can transform a heart, but most "players" are probably not actively seeking God's will in their lives. Being a "player" is not being respectful of you. Even if he tells you, "she means nothing", when speaking of the other girl...You deserve better. You deserve a guy who is faithful to one girl at a time. If you are that girl... great! If it's another girl...great! He needs to be honest and faithful with one girl at a time to be worthy of your attention and loyalty. Again, you deserve to be treated with this kind of respect.

Read 1 Peter 1:14-16

> *[4] As obedient children, do not conform to the evil desires you had when you lived in ignorance. [15] But just as he who called you is holy, so be holy in all you do; [16] for it is written: "Be holy, because I am holy."*[a][b]

Colossians 3:9-10

> *Do not lie to each other, since you have taken off your old self with its practices [10] and have put on the new self, which is being renewed in knowledge in the image of its Creator.* [c]

---

a Lev. 11:44, 45; 19:2; 20:7
b *The Holy Bible : New International Version*. electronic ed. Grand Rapids : Zondervan, 1996, c1984, S. 1 Pe 1:14-16
c *The Holy Bible : New International Version*. electronic ed. Grand Rapids : Zondervan, 1996, c1984, S. Col 3:9-10

Michele Corgiat

Thought of the day:
How is being holy and obedient to God being respectful of yourself?

Day 4
Swine kind #4: The Hostage Taker

Have you ever met somebody, girl or guy, who you really didn't want to hurt. They seem fragile. The "hostage taker" takes this fragile state to the next level. They may actually make statements such as, "If you break up with me, I'm going to kill myself". These are the guys who always seem to have some kind of drama in their lives and you get sucked into rescuing or "being there" for them. I'm not saying that it's inappropriate to help a friend out, or to be supportive of a boyfriend. The challenge comes when a person becomes so involved in the other person's problems that they lose sight of their own needs, responsibilities, and boundaries. When a person threatens to "kill themselves" if you make a choice to leave the relationship, don't take it upon yourself to "save" him. Don't take it upon yourself to be his counselor, pastor, or parent. He needs some serious help. He may be using this threat to keep control of you, to get attention, or because he is seriously depressed and suicidal. Do you want to be the one to find out if he's serious? As mature as you may believe you are, this is an adult issue that needs some serious guidance and intervention. You are not the person to help the boy, and it's not fair of him to put that kind of pressure on you.

Read Romans 12:2-8

Do not conform any longer to the pattern of this world, but be transformed by the renewing of your mind. Then you will be able to test and approve what God's will is—his good, pleasing and perfect will. ³ For by the grace given me I say to every one of you: Do not think of yourself more highly than you ought, but rather think of yourself with sober judgment, in accordance with the measure of faith God has given you. ⁴ Just as each of us has one body with many members, and these members do not all have the same function, ⁵ so in Christ we who are many form one body, and each member belongs to all the others. ⁶ We have different gifts, according to the grace given us. If a man's gift is prophesying, let *him use it in proportion to his ^a faith. ⁷ If it is serving, let him serve; if it is teaching, let him teach; ⁸ if it is encouraging, let him encourage; if it is contributing to the needs of others, let him give generously; if it is leadership, let him govern diligently; if it is showing mercy, let him do it cheerfully.*

Thought of the day:
Have you every known somebody, male or female, who seeks out attention by using drama?

_____

_____

Romans 12:2-8 speaks about how God has gifted and equipped each of his people differently. In what way can you best deal with a person who causes so much drama?

_____

_____

---

a   Or *in agreement with the*

Day 5
Swine Kind #5: Liar, Liar, Pants on Fire!

To be brutally honest, there are those individuals out there who can't tell the truth if their life depended on it. Beware of the boy who weaves great stories and tells tall tales. Throughout all of my work as a counselor, I can tell you one of the basic relationship rules that I've learned…a relationship can not be healthy if there is dishonesty in it. Honesty is a two way street, however.

I wouldn't recommend telling every thought that comes through your head. God has provided us with "filters" to help us determine what should leave our mouth and what shouldn't. "Filtering" is a complex task and may take a lifetime to master. Some individuals struggle and either say every thought, feeling or idea that they experience, or they filter too much by not communicating enough. We sometimes learn how to use these filters through trial and error. Every husband and wife will be able to tell you things they "regretted" saying…and most can tell you about things they probably should have spoken up about sooner. Honesty is the best policy but you also need to use wisdom. A guy who is trying to impress you with his concoction of lies ends up being a pretty big disappointment. If he would be genuine and real, he would earn much more respect, proving himself trustworthy.

Read Proverbs 12:17

> *He that* speaketh truth sheweth forth righteousness: but a false witness deceit[a]
>
> There is that speaketh like the piercings of a sword: but the tongue of the wise *is* health.
>
> [19] The lip of truth shall be established for ever: but a lying tongue *is* but for a moment.

---

a *The Holy Bible : King James Version.* electronic ed. of the 1769 edition of the 1611 Authorized Version. Bellingham WA : Logos Research Systems, Inc., 1995, S. Pr 12:17

> [20] Deceit *is* in the heart of them that imagine evil: but to the counselors of peace *is* joy.
>
> [21] There shall no evil happen to the just: but the wicked shall be filled with mischief.
>
> [22] Lying lips *are* abomination to the LORD: but they that deal truly *are* his delight.
>
> [23] A prudent man concealeth knowledge: but the heart of fools proclaimeth foolishness.

This scripture is so appropriate for today's study. It covers everything from those who speak deceit to using a wise and truthful tongue. Remember, God requires honesty and integrity from each of us. This is just one way that we can be obedient to Him.

Thought of the day:
How do you determine if somebody is being honest with you?
_____
_____

How do you handle somebody being dishonest? Do you ignore their lies or do you confront their dishonesty?
_____
_____

WEEK 4:
Don't be a vampire girl

Day 1
Sucking the life out of others

Earlier in our study we talked briefly about the drama that we create in relationships. Esther is one of my favorite stories of the Bible. I was once involved in a bible study that looked at the book of Esther verse by verse. It was better than any soap opera you could ever watch on television. It's a story of betrayal and loyalty, big egos and humbleness, anxiety and courage. Isn't that what dating is? However, not EVERYONE wants to hear all of the sordid details of your life, especially guys. If you listen to guys in your life, you will notice that they speak very little of drama, and quite frankly, they are not interested in yours. Facing the hard facts that guys are made differently than girls in their thought process is sometimes impossible. If you ask a girl to describe the perfect guy, most likely she will describe another girl. We think and act differently. We enjoy drama. Who do you think they make all of the "chick flicks" for? CHICKS!!!! They make sci-fi, action, shoot 'em up films for guys (remember they are into heroes).

When you pour all of your drama out onto a "friend" whether it's a girl or guy, you are draining that person. Not to say that you can't talk about what may be bothering you…but beware of overloading someone. I know that we need to talk to someone about what is going on in our lives. You may often hear churches say, "Take it to the Lord". Even though this phrase seems so cliché, it's true.

Michele Corgiat

Read Psalms 55:22

> *Cast your cares on the* Lord
> *and he will sustain you;*
> *he will never let the righteous fall.* [a]

Thought of the day:
What problems have you talked to your friends about lately?

_____

_____

What problems have you talked to God about?

_____

_____

Have you ever "sucked" the life out of a relationship because you shared too much?

_____

_____

---

a *The Holy Bible : New International Version.* electronic ed. Grand Rapids : Zondervan, 1996, c1984, S. Ps 55:22

Day 2
Needy is as Needy Does

What is a needy person? More specifically, what defines a needy girl? We all have needs. I have a need for "social interaction". I desire, however, to chat with my best friend about good times and bad times. First thing we need to do is distinguish between our needs and wants. Secondly, we need to decide, out of all of our wants, what is a priority. If we "need" everything we want, we will never feel satisfied. A needy girl is seen as somebody who is never satisfied.

Do you remember the last time you had your favorite meal? You may have eaten until you couldn't eat any more. You felt satisfied. Satisfaction can feel peaceful, full, pleasurable, and calming.

As we learn to depend on God to provide for our needs, and not other people, He will bring healing, an encouraging word, and answers. And I promise, His answers are always perfect. Just a word of warning! He may not always answer in your timing, and His answer may not always be the answer that you are looking for.

Read Deuteronomy 32:4
> *He is the Rock, his works are perfect,*
> *and all his ways are just.*
> *A faithful God who does no wrong,*
> *upright and just is he.* [a]

Thought of the day:
Take a moment to distinguish between your needs and your desires.

---

[a] *The Holy Bible : New International Version.* electronic ed. Grand Rapids : Zondervan, 1996, c1984, S. Dt 32:4

Michele Corgiat

Do you ever feel satisfied in relationships or friendships?
_____
_____

What do you do when you feel satisfied?
_____
_____

Day 3
Afraid of Being Rejected

Nobody likes being rejected. The fear of rejection comes to us when we are pretty young. It's related to the fear of abandonment which develops when we are infants. In the perfect world, we develop a security that those we love will not abandon us or reject us. Reality is, however, that when we are small, we begin to experience rejection. Two little girls are playing on the playground. One of them says, "You can't be my friend anymore because you're _____ (fill in the blank)". Later on when the little girl has grown to middle school age and has a huge crush on a boy, he rejects her. This junior higher grows into a senior in high school. She is giving a speech in class and kids are laughing in the back of the classroom. She takes this on as people rejecting her and judging her.

What do we do with this fear of rejection? Do we build a wall around us, dig a moat, and have guards standing watch to protect ourselves? Do we attach ourselves to every person that shows any interest in our lives until we become so "needy" that we drive everybody away? Believe it or not, there is a happy medium.

I think the best example to use would be the life of Jesus Christ. He came to earth and experienced rejection from birth. He had people who loved him and cared for him, but there was a king who wanted to kill him when he was only an infant. As he grew into middle school age, his parents took him to the temple where again, he had followers and believers at such a young age, but the Pharisees were not too sure about this young boy who taught in "their place". After Jesus began his ministry, everywhere he went there were those who loved him and those who resented and rejected him. He was rejected by his very own culture, people, and government until it cost him his life. Do we ever read about Jesus hiding from his enemy? Do we ever see him become emotionally detached from others? Does Jesus ever get defensive and guarded? No. He knew what his role was. He knew he had a purpose and that rejection was actually part of that purpose.

The truth is, people judge. People reject. It's up to us as to whether we "own" others judgment of ourselves or whether we keep our eyes on the greater purpose. Each of us has a choice as to how we will handle rejection. The first step is to identify anything in your life that may actually need to be changed or dealt with. If you are being rejected because you gossip about your friends…you need to stop gossiping. Once you change a behavior that needs changing, seek God's opinion and acceptance. When we can accept the lovely person that God created, we can disregard the judgments from others.

Read Deuteronomy 31:6
Be strong and courageous. Do not be afraid or terrified because of them, for the LORD *your God goes with you; he will never leave you nor forsake you."* [a]

Thought of the day:
Are you ever afraid of being rejected?
_____
_____

What do you do to "guard your heart" and is it healthy?
_____
_____

---

a *The Holy Bible : New International Version.* electronic ed. Grand Rapids : Zondervan, 1996, c1984, S. Dt 31:6

Day 4
Failed Expectations

Life is full of expectations. On a daily basis you have expectations which are usually met. You may expect that when you awake in the morning, the sun will be up in the sky to greet you. We often expect that when we flip a light switch, electricity will turn on the light. When our expectations are not met, we respond in a variety of ways depending on the consequences of the situation. If I'm expecting my garage door to open when I press the button and it doesn't, I may become quite frustrated if I'm running late to an appointment. However, if I am having a relaxing day with no rush to be anywhere, I may feel only mildly inconvenienced.

We also have expectations within relationships. Many girls find themselves greatly disappointed when their expectations are not met in a relationship. Some expectations are realistic while others may purely be fantasy. Perhaps they have set their expectations too high or their partner has failed. We are human and will fail, and so will your boyfriend or someday husband. Communicating our expectations sometimes remedies this situation. For example, one of the many lessons that I'm sure I failed to learn growing up was to allow a man to open the car door for a lady. I had a good male friend who was upset by this fact. We spent a lot of time together, driving around, and he waited a year before communicating that it bothered him that I didn't allow him to get the car door. Through communication of his expectation, I was able to learn and accommodate his value system. When we communicate expectations, we are showing respect for the other person and for ourselves.

What are your expectations of God? Sometimes we don't think of God in those terms but you do have expectations of Him. You may expect Him to be this Almighty God who has nothing to do with your everyday life. That can be an unrealistic expectation. He is always involved, even if you don't see him directly. On the other hand, you may expect God to take care of everything while you just sit back and watch. Granted, God is in charge and His plan is forever moving forward, however, remember His expectations. He expects you to obey Him, praise Him, and give Him glory!

Read Jeremiah 29:11
> For I know the plans I have for you," declares the LORD, "plans to prosper you and not to harm you, plans to give you hope and a future.[a]

I would like you to take just a moment to remember a story from the Bible. The children of Israel were brought out of Egypt and on their way to the "Promised Land". This land was actually "promised" to the Israelites, but due to their disobedience, they had to wander around the wilderness for 40 years. God made them wait. I love Christmas because of all of the "promised" gifts. How much patience we have to show in waiting for the day we can open our presents! How much more patience must we have to wait for the gifts that God has planned for us!

Thought of the day:
How do you communicate your expectations to others?
_____
_____

What is your expectation of God?
_____
_____

Do you wait for His gifts and promises?
_____
_____

---

a *The Holy Bible : New International Version.* electronic ed. Grand Rapids : Zondervan, 1996, c1984, S. Je 29:11

Day 5
Leave Your Bags at the Door

Through life experiences, good and bad, we pick up "baggage" along the way. Baggage can be judgments, assumptions, self-talk, or messages we get from others. For example, if I was bitten by a dog when I was a child, the baggage that travels with me through life may be a fear of dogs. I may assume that all dogs bite. Relationships also cause us to pick up baggage along the way. Maybe you liked a guy and he commented about your ears being small and then later on broke your heart. You may become overly concerned about your ears because you assume that's why he broke up with you. Your self-talk about your ears may become overwhelmingly negative due to a message that one person gave to you. The next guy you date is blindsided when you may disagree about where to go for dinner and you tearfully blurt out, "it's because my ears are too small, isn't it!" Sister… that is most definitely some baggage. And baggage can hurt and even destroy individual and relationships.

The good news is that you can get rid of unwanted baggage; let go of false messages and lies. Maybe you have known somebody who was just mean and cruel. A message that we sometimes tell ourselves after being in a bad relationship is, "I deserved it". You can choose not to believe that lie by battling it with an opposite message, "nobody deserves to be treated badly." When you continue to fight these negative messages that we tell ourselves, we slowly but surely let go of the baggage.

Another way we can let go of the unwanted baggage is to give it away. There is only one person I know that is glad to take it off your hands and that is God. It's up to you to ask him to take it from you and then to leave it with him. Sometimes we are caught in the trap of giving it away…and then taking right back.

Michele Corgiat

Read Matthew 11:28-30

> *Come to me, all you who are weary and burdened, and I will give you rest.* ^{29} *Take my yoke upon you and learn from me, for I am gentle and humble in heart, and you will find rest for your souls.* ^{30} *For my yoke is easy and my burden is light."* [a]

Thought of the day:
God wants to come along side you and help you in all of your struggles. What struggles or baggage do you need to give to God?

_____

_____

What baggage do you keep giving to Him and then taking back?

---

a   *The Holy Bible : New International Version.* electronic ed. Grand Rapids : Zondervan, 1996, c1984, S. Mt 11:28-30

WEEK 5:

Day 1
Twitterpated vs. love

What is Twitterpated? You know that feeling you get when you really like a guy. Hate to tell you, but that's not love. When you meet a guy that you are interested in, you may experience excitement, nervousness, and feel sparkly and sparky. It is attraction, romance, lust, but definitely not love. It's the feeling you need at the beginning of a relationship to want to get to know each other. Sometimes we misinterpret this feeling as "falling in love". On the other hand, it's at this stage that we may have an argument or disagreement and we think that the world has come to an end. Our emotions seem magnified and our feelings are raw. Some people think that if that feeling wears off that you have "fallen out of love". Remember that roller coaster ride I talked about earlier? The excitement will always wear off as we get more comfortable with another person. That's a good thing. If you always were experiencing feelings of nervousness, excitement and anxiety in a relationship, you would be exhausted! As you get to know a person, and learn their habits, responses, likes and dislikes, they do get more predictable. There is a sense of familiarity in the relationship and familiarity can breed comfort. A good word to describe a long term, unwavering love is "steadfast" love. We can experience the steadfast love God has for us. No matter what we do, He always will love us. No strings attached!

Read Psalms 89:1
> *I will sing of the **steadfast love** of the Lord, forever; with my mouth I will make known your faithfulness to all generations.* *

Lamentations 3:22
> *The **steadfast love** of the Lord never ceases; his mercies never come to an end*

Michele Corgiat

Proverbs 3:3
> *Let not **steadfast love** and faithfulness forsake you; bind them around your neck; write them on the tablet of your heart.*

Thought of the day:
Is it possible for us to experience a true steadfast love for somebody or is steadfast love something we can only attempt to possess for somebody?

Day 2
Love Is As Love Does

Have you ever asked the question, what is love? We tend to throw the "love" word around a lot. You hear people say, "I love pizza", "I love my car", or "I love your shirt". If you look in the Merriam-Webster dictionary you will find love defined as *1 a (1)*: strong affection for another arising out of kinship or personal ties <maternal love for a child> *(2)*: attraction based on sexual desire: affection and tenderness felt by lovers *(3)*: affection based on admiration, benevolence, or common interests <love for his old schoolmates> **b**: an assurance of love <give her my love>

This definition gives you the idea that love is a feeling. Our society tells us that we can "fall in love" and "fall out of love". But, what does the Bible say love is?

Read I Corinthians 13:4-6

⁴ Love is patient, love is kind. It does not envy, it does not boast, it is not proud. ⁵ It is not rude, it is not self-seeking, it is not easily angered, it keeps no record of wrongs. ⁶ Love does not delight in evil but rejoices with the truth. ⁷ It always protects, always trusts, always hopes, always perseveres. [a]

According to this passage, love is not a feeling but a posture of the heart born out in action. Love is…consistent. It's not always passionate, romantic, or exciting. Love is sticking it out even when he stinks from doing yard work, disagrees with you about what to watch on TV, or doesn't communicate in your language.

Love is about commitment despite imperfections and the goal is for that love to go both ways in a relationship.

---

a   *The Holy Bible : New International Version.* electronic ed. Grand Rapids : Zondervan, 1996, c1984, S. 1 Co 13:4-7

Michele Corgiat

Read Song of Solomon 8:6-7

> *Place me like a seal over your heart,*
> *like a seal on your arm;*
> *for love is as strong as death,*
> *its jealousy [a] unyielding as the grave.[b]*
> *It burns like blazing fire,*
> *like a mighty flame.[c]*
> *[7] Many waters cannot quench love;*
> *rivers cannot wash it away.[d]*

Thought of the day:
Have you ever experienced biblical love for anybody?

_____

_____

How can the love described above be used?

_____

_____

---

a Or *ardor*
b Hebrew *Sheol*
c Or / *like the very flame of the* L<small>ORD</small>
d *The Holy Bible : New International Version.* electronic ed. Grand Rapids : Zondervan, 1996, c1984, S. So 8:6-7

Day 3
Waiting on God

If you have never been "in love" with somebody or had somebody "love" you, all is not lost. These things really do take time. Remembering that God's timing is best can be a struggle. Let's explore what "waiting on God" really looks like.

Read Psalms 31:24

> ^a*Be strong, and let your heart take courage,*
> *all you who wait for the* L<small>ORD</small>*!* [b]

If you look up this same scripture in several other versions, the word wait is substituted with the word "hope".

Read Psalms 33:20

> *We wait in hope for the* L<small>ORD</small>*;*
> *he is our help and our shield.* [c]

Micah 7:7

> *But as for me, I watch in hope for the* L<small>ORD</small>*,*
> *I wait for God my Savior;*
> *my God will hear me.* [d]

Again, we see wait and hope together!

---

a   See Ps. 27:14
b   *The Holy Bible : English Standard Version.* Wheaton : Standard Bible Society, 2001, S. Ps 31:24
c   *The Holy Bible : New International Version.* electronic ed. Grand Rapids : Zondervan, 1996, c1984, S. Ps 33:20
d   *The Holy Bible : New International Version.* electronic ed. Grand Rapids : Zondervan, 1996, c1984, S. Mic 7:7

Michele Corgiat

Read Isaiah 30:18

> *Yet the LORD longs to be gracious to you;*
> *he rises to show you compassion.*
> *For the LORD is a God of justice.*
> *Blessed are all who wait for him!* [a]

I know that sometimes we get discouraged because others around us may be in relationships and are living the lives that we desire. God is actively working on you and possibly through you. Don't be discouraged. When you feel down, remember that God's plan for you is better than anything that you can plan yourself. Just wait on Him!

Thought of the day:
How is your patience level?

_____

_____

Does waiting come easy for you?

_____

_____

How have you seen God working in your life?

_____

_____

Make a list of what God has done or provided for you.

_____

_____

---

[a] *The Holy Bible : New International Version.* electronic ed. Grand Rapids : Zondervan, 1996, c1984, S. Is 30:18

Day 4
Broken Hearts and Shattered Dreams

Suffering a broken heart is so painful. If you haven't suffered a broken heart yet, odds are you will. I'd like to express my empathy and sympathy because I know that it will hurt your heart. So many times in life, we may be traveling along assuming that all is right in the world. Then we get broadsided by what feels like a train. When you are injured you have choices and what you choose to do with your hurts is key.

<u>Revenge</u>
Hurt and Anger seem to be best friends. Where one is, you often find the other. When we have been hurt by somebody, we want the other person to feel our pain. What good does hurting somebody else do? Nothing. It only produces wounds and enemies for everyone involved.

<u>Mope</u>
There is most definitely a time in your sadness and grief that you will feel sorry for yourself. And you are allowed to do this…for a moment. Don't let your sadness take over your life. Nobody wants to hang out with an Eeyore! If you allow your broken heart to run your life, you will get stuck in your emotional and spiritual pain rather than continue growing.

<u>Ignore</u>
NO!!! Ignoring your pain doesn't heal it. Think about a person who has a serious injury. If they just ignore the pain and don't deal with the cause, the wound can get infected and lead to death. Not that having your heart broken is going to kill you physically, but by ignoring your pain, you may be causing a part of you to emotionally die.

<u>Working through grief</u>

When we experience a loss we go through the grieving process. In a book by *Elizabeth Kubler-Ross'*, "On Death and Dying." , grief is broken down into 5 stages.

- **D**enial (this isn't *happening* to me!)
- **A**nger (why is this happening to *me?*)
- **B**argaining (I promise I'll be a better person *if*...)
- **D**epression (I don't *care* anymore)
- **A**cceptance (*I'm ready* for whatever comes)

Allowing yourself to get through these stages without focusing on just one stage will help you deal with your broken heart and when you get to the stage of acceptance, you will be able to move forward and give God the praise. I've included the story of Lazarus. It's a great example of people grieving a loss and God's plan being greater than our earthly plans.

Read John 11:17-43

[17] On his arrival, Jesus found that Lazarus had already been in the tomb for four days. [18] Bethany was less than two miles [a] from Jerusalem, [19] and many Jews had come to Martha and Mary to comfort them in the loss of their brother. [20] When Martha heard that Jesus was coming, she went out to meet him, but Mary stayed at home. [21] "Lord," Martha said to Jesus, "if you had been here, my brother would not have died. [22] But I know that even now God will give you whatever you ask." [23] Jesus said to her, "Your brother will rise again." [24] Martha answered, "I know he will rise again in the resurrection at the last day." [25] Jesus said to her, "I am the resurrection and the life. He who believes in me will live, even though he dies; [26] and whoever lives and believes in me will never die. Do you believe this?" [27] "Yes, Lord," she told him, "I believe that you are the Christ,[b] the Son of God, who was to come into the world." [28] And after she had said this, she went back and called her sister Mary aside. "The Teacher is here," she said, "and is asking for you." [29] When Mary heard this, she got up quickly and went to him. [30] Now Jesus had not yet entered the village, but was still at the place where Martha had met him. [31] When the Jews who had been with Mary in the house,

---

a   Greek *fifteen stadia* (about 3 kilometers)
b   Or *Messiah*

comforting her, noticed how quickly she got up and went out, they followed her, supposing she was going to the tomb to mourn there. ³² *When Mary reached the place where Jesus was and saw him, she fell at his feet and said, "Lord, if you had been here, my brother would not have died."* ³³ *When Jesus saw her weeping, and the Jews who had come along with her also weeping, he was deeply moved in spirit and troubled.* ³⁴ *"Where have you laid him?" he asked.*
"Come and see, Lord," they replied.
³⁵ *Jesus wept.*
³⁶ *Then the Jews said, "See how he loved him!"* ³⁷ *But some of them said, "Could not he who opened the eyes of the blind man have kept this man from dying?"* ³⁸ *Jesus, once more deeply moved, came to the tomb. It was a cave with a stone laid across the entrance.* ³⁹ *"Take away the stone," he said.*
"But, Lord," said Martha, the sister of the dead man, "by this time there is a bad odor, for he has been there four days."
⁴⁰ *Then Jesus said, "Did I not tell you that if you believed, you would see the glory of God?"*
⁴¹ *So they took away the stone. Then Jesus looked up and said, "Father, I thank you that you have heard me.* ⁴² *I knew that you always hear me, but I said this for the benefit of the people standing here, that they may believe that you sent me."*
⁴³ *When he had said this, Jesus called in a loud voice, "Lazarus, come out!"* ⁴⁴ *The dead man came out, his hands and feet wrapped with strips of linen, and a cloth around his face. Jesus said to them, "Take off the grave clothes and let him go."* [a]

Thought of the day:
What losses have you experienced?
_____

_____

What choice(s) did you make in response to your hurting heart?
_____

_____

---

a   *The Holy Bible : New International Version.* electronic ed. Grand Rapids : Zondervan, 1996, c1984, S. Jn 11:17-44

Day 5
Till Death do us part

When and who to marry!?! Hopefully this book has provided some thoughts and tools for you to help in eventually making this decision. Don't marry because of pressure. Don't marry out of desperation. Be prayerful. Be hopeful. Be wise.

Marriage was not created to make you happy.
Don't get me wrong, a marriage can be very rewarding, but it's not created to make you a whole person. In marriage, we often give much more than we receive. Remember, you are to be a helpmate.

We are called to die to ourselves daily.
In marriage, you are quite frequently asked to put your own agenda aside for the greater good of your spouse and relationship.

Marriage is designed to reflect God's image.
If you keep this in mind, you will be less judgmental of your spouse and more tolerant of differences you may have.

I know that finding your prince may be the desire of your heart. Being open to God's desires for you will bless you more than any earthly relationship. Marriage can be a blessing but building a Christian marriage and keeping it strong requires work. Although most of the young ladies reading this may not be ready for marriage, here are some tools to keep in your "relationship tool belt" for the future.

- Pray together
- Read the Bible together
- Make important decisions together
- Go to church together
- Serve others together

- Have fun together
- Spend romantic time together

Read Genesis 2:18

> *The L*ORD *God said, "It is not good for the man to be alone. I will make a helper suitable for him."* [a]

Genesis 1:27

> *So God created man in his own image,*
> *in the image of God he created him;*
> *male and female he created them.* [b]

Thought of the day:
Do you know any couples that you would consider to have a strong Christian marriage based on this information?

_____

_____

List how this couple may be reflecting God's image.

_____

---

a   *The Holy Bible : New International Version.* electronic ed. Grand Rapids : Zondervan, 1996, c1984, S. Ge 2:18

b   *The Holy Bible : New International Version.* electronic ed. Grand Rapids : Zondervan, 1996, c1984, S. Ge 1:27

WEEK 6:
How do you get back on track if you already took the wrong road?

Day 1
Reexamine

Somebody once asked me if I thought they were wrong in reexamining their relationship. I believe it's wrong not to reexamine your relationships, your actions and behavior, and your life in general. Not that we can undo choices that have already been made, but by reexamining our life, we can make sure we are living our life according to how God would have us live. During our relationships, we should be continuing to grow as individuals as well as in our relationships. If we look at relationships like a tree, baby trees are weak and small. As a tree grows, it hopefully becomes large, strong, beautiful and fruitful. What happens when we don't take care of that tree and examine it from time to time? The tree may get infested by bugs or disease. If the tree has been planted in an area that doesn't allow for room to grow, the tree's growth is stunted and it's fruitfulness limited.

Read John 15:1-17

I am the true vine, and my Father is the gardener. ² He cuts off every branch in me that bears no fruit, while every branch that does bear fruit he prunes[aa] so that it will be even more fruitful. ³ You are already clean because of the word I have spoken to you. ⁴ Remain in me, and I will remain in you. No branch can bear fruit by itself; it must remain in the vine. Neither can you bear fruit unless you remain in me.

⁵ "I am the vine; you are the branches. If a man remains in me and I in him, he will bear much fruit; apart from me you can do nothing. ⁶ If anyone does not remain in me, he is like a branch that is thrown

---
a The Greek for *prunes* also means *cleans.*

away and withers; such branches are picked up, thrown into the fire and burned. ⁷ If you remain in me and my words remain in you, ask whatever you wish, and it will be given you. ⁸ This is to my Father's glory, that you bear much fruit, showing yourselves to be my disciples. ⁹ "As the Father has loved me, so have I loved you. Now remain in my love. ¹⁰ If you obey my commands, you will remain in my love, just as I have obeyed my Father's commands and remain in his love. ¹¹ I have told you this so that my joy may be in you and that your joy may be complete. ¹² My command is this: Love each other as I have loved you. ¹³ Greater love has no one than this, that he lay down his life for his friends. ¹⁴ You are my friends if you do what I command. ¹⁵ I no longer call you servants, because a servant does not know his master's business. Instead, I have called you friends, for everything that I learned from my Father I have made known to you. ¹⁶ You did not choose me, but I chose you and appointed you to go and bear fruit—fruit that will last. Then the Father will give you whatever you ask in my name. ¹⁷ This is my command: Love each other [a]

Thought Of The Day:
Do you have relationships that have become infected by sin?

_____

_____

Do any of your relationships limit your growth as an individual?

_____

_____

---

a   *The Holy Bible : New International Version.* electronic ed. Grand Rapids : Zondervan, 1996, c1984, S. Jn 15:1-17

Day 2
Relocation

No, you don't have to move. But have you ever noticed that you seem to meet the same kind of guy over and over again? Most likely you continue to fish out of the same pond. Maybe you need to admit that the pond you've been fishing in is actually a swamp. It's time to start fishing in a fresh pond, and I'm not talking about another swamp! Where are you meeting guys? Friends of friends? Parties? Church? School? I've always had a rule of thumb. Don't date a guy if you know up front that you wouldn't consider marrying him. Even if he's the hottest guy on this side of the Mississippi, don't go down that road. Make a detailed list of your desires in the "Mr. Right". This list will help you in determining what is really important to you and what you can let go. For example, it should be a number one priority that he is a Christian, but being able to perform a cartwheel may be negotiable. As you begin to learn what you value in others, you will also learn about yourself. I have included a brief and non-inclusive list of some values that you may want to consider. Please add as many of your own as you can come up with.

- Loves God
- Shares a heart for ministry
- Likes to travel
- Likes animals
- Values family
- Wants/doesn't want kids
- Enjoys same kind of relaxation
- Appreciates music
- Enjoys worship

- Values educated
- Shares work ethic

Finding a guy who has the same value system that you hold is key to a more fulfilling relationship. If you hold different values, these will always be a source of conflict between you. For example, if you hold family as important, but he doesn't, if he values socializing, but you are a homebody, if you hold Jesus as the most valuable person in your life, but he puts Jesus as #2 or #3, this will bring frustration, heartache, and conflict to a relationship. Making your value list will help you weed out the guys who are definitely not for you. If you are hanging out at places that are not where others with your value systems hang, find a new place! Church should not be seen as a "meat market", but you will find others with similar values. Never assume just because they attend a church that they are at the same level of relationship with Christ as you are. Take it slow, and get to know the guy.

Read 2 Corinthians 6:14-17

> Do not be yoked together with unbelievers. For what do righteousness and wickedness have in common? Or what fellowship can light have with darkness? [15] What harmony is there between Christ and Belial[a]? What does a believer have in common with an unbeliever? [16] What agreement is there between the temple of God and idols? For we are the temple of the living God. As God has said: "I will live with them and walk among them, and I will be their God, and they will be my people."[bc]

Thought of the day:
Make a list of your desired qualities in a guy.

_____

_____

Prioritize that list.

How many of these qualities do you hold?

_____

_____

---

a Greek *Beliar*, a variant of *Belial*
b Lev. 26:12; Jer. 32:38; Ezek. 37:27
c *The Holy Bible : New International Version*. electronic ed. Grand Rapids : Zondervan, 1996, c1984, S. 2 Co 6:14-16

Day 3
Repentance

Have you ever been on a trip, or maybe just driving down the road in your town when you realize that you might be lost? You may travel for quite some time before you realize that you are headed in the wrong direction. It's not until you have had the realization that you have to make a very important choice. The choice to turn around.

Sometimes we make really bad choices in our lives. Some we regret more than others. You may find yourself on the relationship road where you are reexamining things and you find that you're going in the wrong direction or possibly on the wrong road all together. Some roads are slippery slopes, while others seem to be rocky and full of pot holes. Even the best of relationships can have their struggles, but I'm talking about when you have realized that you are clearly in the wrong relationship. I have found many young women to be so far down this road and "in love" that they are not sure that they truly want to get on the right road which is the road that God has for them. They make excuses, stay due to insecurities, or don't feel precious enough to be worthy of changing directions.

If you know that you are going down the wrong road, I promise, you will not enjoy that road nearly as much. I may be traveling down the most picturesque and scenic drive in the world, but if I am aware that the road I am on is leading me towards destruction, sooner or later I am not going to enjoy the view. I'm always going to be looking for what is around the next corner and live in fear and unrest. The same will go for you in a relationship that you know is not in God's plan. Maybe you find yourself making bad choices in unhealthy men or participating in sexual sin. The first step to getting in the right direction is admitting that you're going in the wrong direction. If you have gotten lost in a relationship or maybe have sexual sin in your life, you don't have to continue down that road.

How do you turn around when you're lost? How do you know what the right direction is? After you have admitted that you are lost, turning around is sometimes harder that you can imagine. In the Bible, turning completely around is called repentance. It can be a painful process, but that's just what it is…a process. It's turning from you sin and making the right choices and repeating those choices. Sometimes we mess up and we fail. Picking yourself up and making the right choice only helps you get going in the right direction. Sometimes these choices are huge and sometimes small. Some of the bigger choices could be breaking up with a guy, taking him off your Facebook page, choosing to not call him when you are feeling down, reaching out to other women for support, and most importantly, calling out to your Abba Father when you are feeling alone. Giving you time to heal from a broken heart is also a good choice. As previously said, we are not in a rush to find "Mr. Right". God's timing is perfect and he will bring the perfect relationship in His time.

Read I John 1:9
If we confess our sins, he is faithful and just and will forgive us our sins and purify us from all unrighteousness [a]

This Scripture may be familiar to you. This Scripture is used by many to talk about how God does forgive us. Now read this scripture in context with how it was used.

I John 1:8-10
[8] If we claim to be without sin, we deceive ourselves and the truth is not in us. [9] If we confess our sins, he is faithful and just and will forgive us our sins and purify us from all unrighteousness. [10] If we claim we have not sinned, we make him out to be a liar and his word has no place in our lives. [b]

Thought of the day:
Sometimes admitting that we are going down the wrong road is tough. It takes some humility. Identify areas of your life that may be in sin.

---

a   *The Holy Bible : New International Version.* electronic ed. Grand Rapids : Zondervan, 1996, c1984, S. 1 Jn 1:9
b   *The Holy Bible : New International Version.* electronic ed. Grand Rapids : Zondervan, 1996, c1984, S. 1 Jn 1:8-10

The purpose of making a list is not to cause you guilt and shame. It's to help you identify areas that you need to turn over to God. How can you turn these areas over to Him?

_____

_____

_____

_____

_____

Day 4
Restoration

Luke 7:36-50 tells a story about a woman who was a "sinner". It's assumed that in Biblical times a "sinner woman" was a woman who was known for her sexual sins. She may have been known as a "harlot" or in today's world, a "hoochy mama". The Pharisees who had invited Jesus to eat with them couldn't believe that Christ was allowing such a woman to wash his feet. Although the Pharisees wanted Christ to reject her, Christ did not rebuke her and turn her away. She was repentant, and humbled herself before Jesus, washing his feet with her hair and her tears. Did he laugh at her? Did he tell her to get away from him? Did he withdraw from her? No, he accepted her humbleness and blessed her. Although, you may have allowed yourself to make bad choices in your love life and may have sexual sin, God still loves you and wants you to experience his grace. He continues to believe that you are special and that you are worthy of his blessings and forgiveness. The next step is to forgive yourself.

Read Ephesians 4:24
> *and to put on the new self,* **created** *after the likeness of God in true righteousness and holiness.*

Psalm 23:3
> *He restores my soul.*
> *He guides me in paths of righteousness*
> *for his name's sake.*

Thought of the day:
When we try on the new pair of shoes, how often do we forget about the old pair that is left in our closet?

_____

_____

Why is it so much harder to put on a "new self"?

_____
_____
_____
_____
_____

Day 5
Reconnecting

This may sound totally crazy…but once you have accepted Christ's forgiveness and in turn forgiven yourself, you now need to reconnect with the princess inside of you. We all have dreams that we have to put aside or let go of as we grow and mature, but you may reconnect with your dream of finding Mr. Right. Finding that person that shows you the love and respect that God desires for you.

It's okay to be scared, scared that maybe you won't find the right guy, scared that you will be rejected or abandoned, scared that you may fall into old patterns and fall into another bad or unhealthy relationship. Remember! You get to make the choice of the person you are with and how you will be with that person. You get to choose!

Your actions are the proof of your obedience to God, proof that God is powerful and that in control. We can see these examples of obedience throughout God's Word.

- David and Goliath – God had little David fight giant Goliath… with a slingshot! How often do we feel unprepared, weak, and non-soldier like, standing before a giant, scary situation and God tells us to move forward? Do you?

- Abraham and Isaac – God told Abraham to take his son to a mountain top and sacrifice him. Abraham didn't argue… he said, "Yes Lord". God stopped him. Do you submissively obey God, even when he is asking you to do something incomprehensible?

- Moses – God told him to lead the children of Israel out of Egypt. Moses was one man and often felt alone. God continually spoke to Moses, and Moses obeyed. Do you spend time with God and ask Him what He thinks?

There are so many more examples of when we are obedient to God, even when we feel that His request may seem unreasonable, scary, and out of our league, that He shows His greatness, power and mercy through His will. It takes faith in the unseen. Don't make your faith invisible by not taking action.

Read Philippians 5:2-8
> *⁵ Your attitude should be the same as that of Christ Jesus:*
> *⁶ Who, being in very nature[a] God,*
> *did not consider equality with God something to be grasped,*
> *⁷ but made himself nothing,*
> *taking the very nature [b] of a servant,*
> *being made in human likeness.*
> *⁸ And being found in appearance as a man,*
> *he humbled himself*
> *and became obedient to death—*
> *even death on a cross![c]*

Thought of the day:
What actions are you taking in obedience to God?

_____

_____

As we conclude this study, my hope for you, whether a teen, a young adult, or woman who is still searching for her "happily ever after", is that you make God your priority. That He will become your happily ever after for eternity. This life is temporal. The heartache and pain, the joy and happiness are but specks in eternity. We stand in the hope of our Abba Father's comfort and Almighty God's victory over sin.

May your light shine and give God the glory for what He does for you and through you!

_____

a   Or *in the form of*
b   Or *the form*
c   *The Holy Bible : New International Version.* electronic ed. Grand Rapids : Zondervan, 1996, c1984, S. Php 2:5-8

CPSIA information can be obtained
at www.ICGtesting.com
Printed in the USA
FSHW012130111021
85408FS